# warkworth
Ian Smith

Thanks to all those who have helped, with information and hospitality.


to C


The 'Walk' maps are based on Ordnance Survey maps:
at about 1: 22000, based on Pathfinder 501, (1989);
at about 1: 45000, based on Landranger 81, (1981)
with the permission of the Controller of Her Majesty's
Stationery Office.   © Crown Copyright.

First published in Great Britain by Sandhill Press Limited,
17 Castle Street, Warkworth, MORPETH, Northumberland,
NE65 0UW, 1990

Copyright © Ian Smith 1990.


First impression 1990
Second impression 1993
Reprinted in 2015


ISBN 978 0 9931161 2 4


All rights reserved. No part of this publication may be
reproduced, stored in a retrieval system or transmitted
in any form or by any means, electronic, mechanical,
photocopying, recording or otherwise, without the prior
permission of the copyright holder.

Printed by Azure Printing

# Contents                                   Warkworth

| | |
|---|---|
| Town Map. | 2. |
| St. Lawrence's Church. | 4. |
| Warkworth Bridge. | 6. |
| Bridge Street. | 8. |
| Market Place. | 9. |
| Castle Street. | 10. |
| The Castle. | 12. |
| The Butts. | 16. |
| The Burgages Path. | 18. |
| Walk to the Hermitage | 20. |
| The Hermitage | 22. |
| Walk to Warkworth Beach and Harbour | 24. |
| Walk via Amble to Coquet Mouth. | 26. |
| Index and Bibliography | 30. |

Foreword to the 2015 reprint

Much has happened in a quarter century, but Warkworth has remained essentially unchanged. Businesses have come and gone, of course. The Book House has unfortunately gone, as has a tea-room. But now there is an excellent chocolaterie — not to be missed! So this reprint is offered unaltered. Enjoy.
Ian Smith, February 2015.

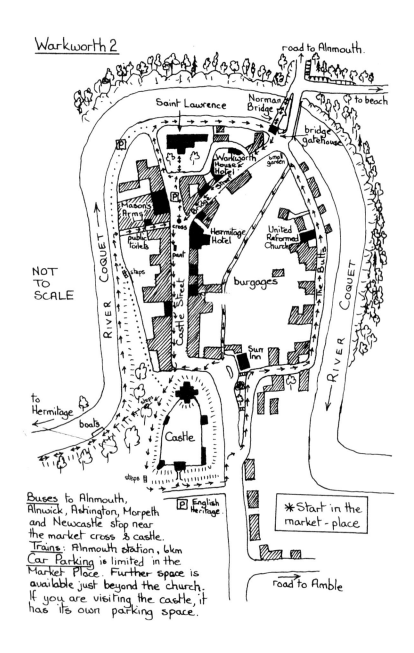

# Warkworth 3

Warkworth town displays the essential characteristics of this border kingdom: a defensive position; a river; a castle and a quiet elegance largely unravaged by English commercialism.
This is a town to enjoy in any season — when a hard frost bites as the sun sinks behind black skeletons of trees beneath an apricot-coloured sky, or when balmy breezes shake the leaves above your rowing boat on a summer day.
Warkworth is Northumbrian.
Warkworth is romantic!

# Warkworth 4 : Saint Lawrence.

As long ago as 737 AD. there was a church of St. Lawrence in Warkworth, but their building was probably destroyed by Danish raids in the ninth century.
A stone church was built — its foundations underlie today's chancel arch. The nave of the present building is Norman. Its function was to protect the people physically as well as spiritually. Note the rather forbidding north wall, with its few, high-set windows. Nevertheless the population, three hundred in all, were massacred in the church during a Scots raid in 1174 AD.
The west tower was added around 1200 AD.
The Percy family extended the church in the fifteenth century, adding the south aisle. This made the church much lighter and brighter, if less secure. (But now the castle was much stronger).

A detailed guide to the church building can be bought inside for a small sum: its purchase may help to keep the fabric up for another nine hundred years.

A peaceful winter evening: St Lawrence.

# Warkworth 5

The <u>chancel arch</u> is a typical Norman semi-circular arch, decorated, and now slightly askew.

Beyond is the <u>Norman chancel</u>, with beautiful vaulting, of a style developed in Durham Cathedral.

The chancel contains parts of early <u>Celtic crosses</u> from the early days of the church.

Near the door is a <u>tomb</u> with the effigy of a knight upon it. The inscription suggests that Sir Hugh died in the Crusades, but the style of armour suggests otherwise. The shield carries the arms of the de Aublyn family of Durham.

> \* After visiting the church go back out of the churchyard and follow the wall to the right, to the riverside, and along to the bridge.

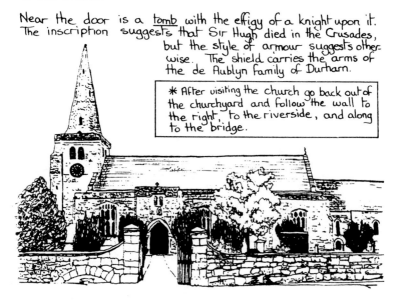

# Warkworth 6

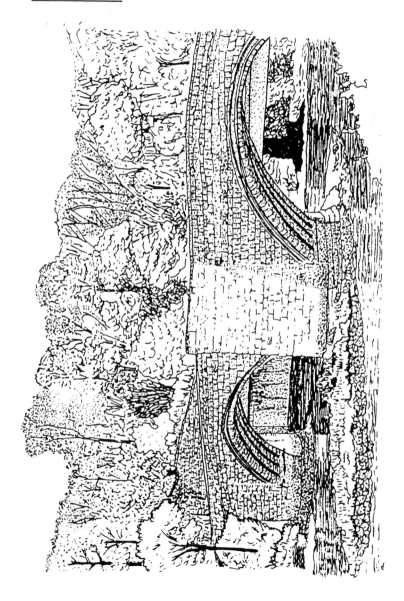

Warkworth 7

The bridge is a widened version of the Norman bridge.
A cross used to stand in the eastern refuge, until it was thrown into the river by "certain idle persons" in 1830. Vandalism is nothing new!
Until the new bridge was built alongside in 1965, all the traffic had to negotiate the gatehouse and narrow bridge. Bus driving must have been interesting!

The gatehouse is most unusual.
Very few towns in England have a fortified bridge. This one was necessary to secure the defensive position of the castle from attack at this point of weakness. It includes a lockup cell, used until not long ago to confine persons arrested for being drunk and disorderly.

# Warkworth 8 : Bridge Street

> ✱ From the gatehouse by the bridge walk into town along Bridge Street to the Market Place.

Bridge Street presents a dour face to arrivals from the north. The dark houses open directly onto the narrow street. It looks and feels rather like a gauntlet to be run to reach the centre of town.

(at the time of writing) Warkworth has five hostelries to cater to the needs of market visitors but also for travellers. Note the openings through into court-yards for stabling. Here horses would be changed for journeys on to Alnwick or Morpeth. Today's travellers also find a welcome.

## Warkworth Inns:

- Warkworth House Hotel (top)
- The Black Bull (above).
- The Hermitage Hotel (right)
- The Mason's Arms (next page)
- The Sun Inn, at the other end of town, next to the castle.

# Market Place

## Warkworth 9

Right here, in 1714, James "the Pretender" was proclaimed as King in England for the first time, at the start of the Jacobite rebellion. The army paused here on its way round Northumberland, recruiting for the Catholic cause, and joined here a party from Scotland. The vicar refused to conduct worship for them, and rode off to inform the authorities in Newcastle.

The Market Cross, (below), dates from 1830. It replaced an earlier cross, dating from 1706, the base and stump of which are now in the castle. The cross is a reminder to traders that God is active in the marketplace as well as in the church.

Market Cross and Castle Street

# Warkworth 10 : Castle Street

* From the market-place walk up the hill towards the castle.

Castle Street is distinctly lighter in tone than Bridge Street. It is wider and more open, to accommodate the market, and it gets the sun more. The trees add their touch of cheer too.
This part of the village has escaped the horrors of high-street modernism and retains its plain Northumbrian style.

The <u>pant</u> (right) is an essential feature for any market. It is inactive at present.

# Warkworth 11

To a passing motorist the village appears to offer little by way of normal commercial facilities. This is partly due to the lack of "standard" shopfronts.

Those on foot can find (at the time of writing)**

- a post-office
- two café/tea-rooms
- two general stores
- an antiques shop
- a gift/crafts shop
- a bookshop (see below)
- five inns (already mentioned)
- two churches (St. Lawrence, Church of England, (United Reformed — on the Butts).
- public toilets (in Hotspur Court, near the market place).
- an art gallery.

What more can you require?

In spring the castle motte at the head of Castle Street is a riot of golden daffodils. — much better than Grasmere.

** The Book House has unfortunately gone, but Warkworth has remained essentially unchanged.

# Warkworth 12 : the Castle

> *  Go round outside the curtain wall of the castle, on the west side. A surfaced footpath (with steps up) takes you to the gatehouse where you can decide whether to visit the interior. English Heritage is custodian of the castle, and makes a charge for visits. They also publish an excellent detailed guidebook.

There had to be a castle at Warkworth. It is on the coastal road, with convenient harbour facilities, and there was that superb defensive position — the horseshoe loop of the river. A mound at the south end closed the ring.
The castle that you see is built up on the original mound, (motte) and courtyard (bailey). The keep is positioned to give the best views up and down-river, and the main street of the town was built under its direct gaze, with the approach from the south-east curving round the bailey.

# Warkworth 13

The curtain walls that surround the bailey date in part from the twelfth century, and, oddly, do not enclose the whole of the original bailey. The castle was strengthened during the twelfth to fifteenth centuries, with further towers, living quarters, a new keep..... It was a notable factor in the struggles between English and Scots.

In 1332 the castle was granted by Edward III to Henry, second Lord Percy of Alnwick. Since then its history has been closely entwined with that of the Northumberland Percys, who for a while chose this as their main residence in preference to Alnwick. Even now they maintain a presence in the keep.

The Percys, including the famous Harry Hotspur who did not live to inherit the Earldom, were pivotal characters in the turbulent times at the start of the fifteenth century. The first Earl, and his son Hotspur, were largely responsible for settling Henry IV on England's throne, and then were instrumental in various attempts to unseat him! Thus Warkworth is the setting for three scenes in William Shakespeare's "Henry the Fourth, Part One". Considering that the Percys had made it both secure and remarkably comfortable, the reference to it as "that worm-eaten hold of ragged stone" was peculiarly inaccurate!

West Postern.

to gatehouse →

to river →

# Warkworth 14: the Castle

The gatehouse is massively impressive. Built in the 13th century it is a superb piece of design and construction. Originally there was a drawbridge: you can see where it fitted up against the gate. Up above are large square holes where the timber galleries were fitted. From these archers, rock-throwers and oil-boilers could fire down on attackers. Even if the enemy passed the gate and portcullis they found out the hard way that there was a second gate, with plenty of nooks for well-protected defenders to add to their misery!

The Lion Tower sports the remains of a splendid Percy Lion, and two coats of arms. Note the Percy crescent with the motto 'Esperance' around the lion's neck. The tower forms an entrance to the Great Hall, the main domestic building.

In the centre of the bailey are the foundations of a Collegiate church, an idea of the first Earl who wanted a college of secular canons here. It was never completed.

## Warkworth 15

The <u>keep</u> is a lovely piece of military architecture, combining strength, defendability and comfort for the occupants together with elegance of shape. (Did you notice the rampant Percy Lion on the face overlooking the town?)

From the keep you can reverse the fine river views, looking downstream to Amble and Coquet Island, and up towards the Hermitage (not itself visible). There is a marvelous view over the town and its burgages. On the south side you look out over the bailey, the curtain walls and other towers, such as the <u>Grey Mare's Tail Tower</u> (below). Can you find the tiny carved crucifixes in this tower?

# Warkworth 16  The Butts

* Make your way from the Castle gateway back round to the top of the town, either back along the path outside the western curtain-wall, or down the Castle drive-way and along the road. Steps go down beside the Sun Inn. (If you are unable to tackle steps use the road). Descend to the riverside and walk along The Butts.

To those expecting the archery grounds of olde England, the <u>Butts</u> may be a disappointment: the name almost certainly refers to the short butte-ends of land left over from the burgages along the riverbank.

But whatever else, this is a place of beauty, with the quiet deep river and the wooded cliffs opposite. Sit on the seat and drink it in.

# Warkworth 17

- The <u>presbyterian church</u> (now United Reformed) dates from 1828.

- The <u>schools</u> are built on the "lord's waste" beside the river. First, near the bridge, the Borough school-house was built by a beneficiary for the town in 1736. This became the school-master's house for the National School, built alongside in 1824.

- The Coquet below Warkworth is an excellent place to see herons, standing quietly in the far shallows stalking their prey, or flapping lazily overhead. But for nearly 4 years, from spring 1973 until Christmas Eve 1976 it was the home for an unusual visitor:
<u>Percy the Pelican</u> became a familiar sight on the river or the cricket field.
Now his stuffed remains may be seen in the Hancock Museum in Newcastle.

# Warkworth 18: the Burgages Path.

**Bridge End House** stands next to the Norman gatehouse. Built in the early eighteenth century, it is easily the most magnificent house in the town. It has managed to retain its iron railings and gate, so many of which went for scrap as a public morale booster during the Second War.

**The burgages** are the long narrow strips of land that stretch all the way from the houses of the town down to the river (apart from the butt-ends already met). This is the mediaeval pattern that has survived until today with remarkably little change, even though the houses in the town have been rebuilt. The best overview of them is from the castle keep, but the path from bridge to castle, a right-of-way for hundreds of years, cuts right across them, cutting the gardens in two. Despite their great length many are kept in immaculate condition — there must be some keen gardeners in Warkworth!

## Warkworth 19.

* Beside the small public garden opposite the bridge gatehouse a path disappears between trees and high walls towards the top of the town. Follow this path between the walls, hedges and fences, enjoying the garden scenes, until you debouch onto the road before the Sun Inn.

Here, at the top of the town, you can decide whether the trip to the Hermitage — or another of the walks out of town — is just the thing to complete your day, or would be better if deferred to a fresh day.

The Sun Hotel

# Warkworth 20: Walk to the Hermitage

Before you set off, do note that the Hermitage is on the far bank of the river, and can only be visited if the English Heritage warden is on duty with his ferry. The Castle folk will tell you the opening days and times. There is a fee for visits to the Hermitage (ferry included!)
Even if the ferry is inoperative, the walk up the river to the landing is charming, at any time of year, with trees, wildlife and woodland flowers as well as the Coquet.

✸ From the castle gateway follow the path round the west curtain wall almost to the town. Just by the west postern turn sharply back down a path to the riverside.
Pass the hire-boat landing, and walk upstream. You will pass Queen Alexandra's Landing, and, round the bend, the concrete outlet for the waterworks above Coquet Lodge. Go on past a stile and join the tarmac track that comes down from Howlet Hall for a few metres until you reach the ferry landing. (All that is visible on the far bank is the hut and landing — the Hermitage is totally hidden by centuries-old yew trees.

2.0 kilometres } Castle to Hermitage
1¼ miles     } and back to town.

# Warkworth 21

- Boats may be hired (in season) for you to row upstream (or down). Note, however, that you are not allowed to land on the Hermitage bank from hire boats.

- Queen Alexandra's landing stage was built especially for her visit. For some years the Hermitage ferry ran from here.

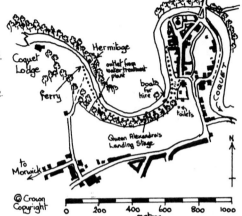

*Return to Warkworth by the same route

# Warkworth 22: The Hermitage.

> The Hermitage is in the care of English Heritage, and may only be visited when the custodian/ferryman is present. There is an entrance fee, and an excellent detailed guide-book.

Reading the guidebooks and histories of the Hermitage can not convey the sense of sheer romance that actually being there brings. From the opposite riverbank there is no hint of the site. It is completely hidden behind massive yews, probably as old as the Hermitage itself. But having crossed the river in the ferry — a romantic enough entrance in itself on a good day — you walk along the north bank, past a spring, to enter under the yews into a twilight world.

Up a sweeping stone staircase the chapel doorway is an opening straight into the side of the cliff, flanked by windows of very different sizes. Down below, between cliff and river, the dwelling-house lies a ruin in stone.

- The chapel and sacristy are hewn into the sandstone of the cliff. But this is no rough cave. The masons who built this place created a place of beauty: the chapel has three bays, each with the ceiling carved out to represent vaulting, — although this work was never completed. A doorway just opposite the porch leads through into an inner chamber, the sacristy.

The chapel has several features carved from the rock:
- an altar at the east end, incised with 19th century graffiti;
- an ornate window through into the sacristy, near the altar;
- a south-facing window with remains of carved figures in the recess, possibly a Nativity scene;
- another external window, carved in quatrefoil ✧ shape;
- a doorway into the sacristy, above which is a carved shield which bore the instruments of the Passion: spear, sponge, crown of thorns, nails and the Cross, plus an inscription.
- loopholes in the west wall, once allowing the chapel to be viewed from the solar of the house.

- The living rooms, below the cliff, comprise kitchen, hall and solar. Little remains of the kitchen, at the foot of the stairs, except the circular base of an oven. A stairway, now inaccessible, goes up through a cleft in the rock to reach the site of the hermit's garden.

The hall, which boasts a fine fireplace, has the depth of various floods clearly cut into the stone — living here would have its drawbacks!

The solar was above the hall, and included a chamber cut into the cliff at the west end of the chapel.

# Warkworth 23.

History. The origins of the chapel are not precisely known. The site may well have been an ancient site of worship, like the cup-and-ring marked cliff by the old ford at Morwick, 3km upriver. Here the fresh spring in the cliffs would have been of importance. It is presumed that one of the Lords Percy of Warkworth had the chapel built in the fourteenth century. The Scottish assault on the town in 1341 might explain the interruption of the carving on the chapel vaulting. The Percy family maintained a chaplain here, with a fairly decent living — this was not a retreat into poverty. But by 1567 the family had other interests and the hermitage was mentioned in the estate surveys in the past tense.

There are, of course, various legends of its origin, tales of love and passion, death and remorse — but you would expect that here!

# Warkworth 24.   Walk to Warkworth Beach & Harbour

- **Warkworth Harbour.** Until 1765 the Coquet performed a last loop before entering the sea more or less opposite the road from Warkworth, through the dunes. Beacon Hill used to be on the south side of the river — it still marks the boundary of Amble (As it is now inconveniently sited from Amble's point of view, Beacon Hill was ignored for the Armada 400 celebrations, in favour of a brazier erected next to the new marina). In 1765 the river changed course, and the old harbour silted up. Part of it is sealed in behind Castle's Dike (named after the constructor, not Warkworth Castle). At low tide much of the old harbour is mud-flats, with attendant bird-life.
- **Amble Harbour.** After its change of course the Coquet reached the sea by a variety of routes through the dunes, leaving a series of islands and an unnavigable sand-bar. From 1836 the problem was solved by building the break-waters to channel the river flow. Staithes to handle the coal traffic from Broomhill colliery followed, and the town developed. Now Amble is recovering from the coal traffic, and developing as a resort.

The north breakwater was extensively rebuilt and reinforced during the 1980's, occasioning the temporary road beside Warkworth Harbour, for construction traffic.

7.0 km, (4¼ miles) circular           Warkworth 25.

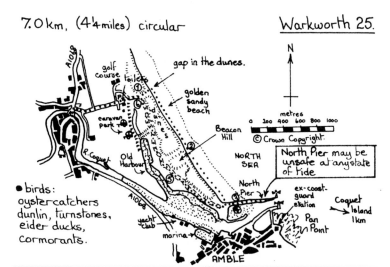

* Cross the Norman bridge and follow the 'Cemetery' sign-post, up the tree-lined side-road to the east. Continue to a cross-roads. (To the south is a caravan park, to the north a golf course). Go straight on, down the path between the car-parks. Pass over the flat area (the old harbour/river mouth) and reach the beach, through a gap in the dunes.
Turn south along the strand of fine sand towards the river-mouth, until you reach the breakwater. Note the warning signs. The track beside the old harbour is not a right of way, but provides a convenient return route. It may be flooded – beware! Note how the high watch-tower of the castle is visible for most of this return walk to the town.

# Warkworth 26    Walk via Amble to Coquet-Mouth.

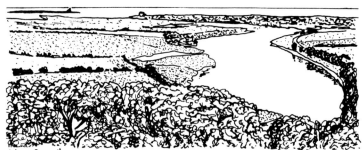

View from the Castle down-river towards Amble and Coquet Island.

* Follow the A1068 road out of Warkworth, past the Castle and down to the riverside. (The footpath along from the Butts, shown on O.S. maps, may exist legally, but not in practice). A decent footpath, separated from the road by a wide verge, takes you alongside the river, downstream past the semi-tidal weir. Continue until you reach a gateway opening on to the Braid.....

Warkworth Castle from the east

# 4.0 km (2½ miles) to Amble South Pier.   Warkworth 27

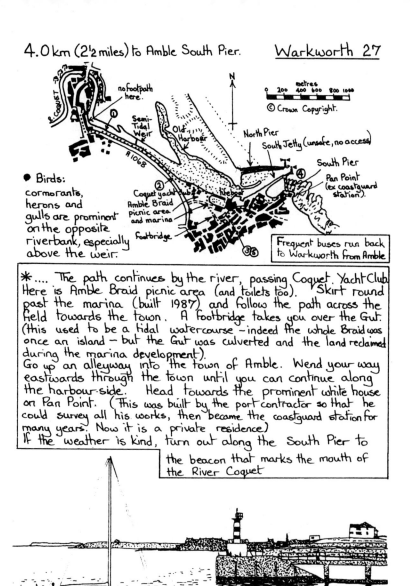

- **Birds:** cormorants, herons and gulls are prominent on the opposite riverbank, especially above the weir.

Frequent buses run back to Warkworth from Amble

*.... The path continues by the river, passing Coquet Yacht Club. Here is Amble Braid picnic area (and toilets too). Skirt round past the marina (built 1987) and follow the path across the field towards the town. A footbridge takes you over the Gut. (This used to be a tidal watercourse — indeed the whole Braid was once an island — but the Gut was culverted and the land reclaimed during the marina development).

Go up an alleyway into the town of Amble. Wend your way eastwards through the town until you can continue along the harbour-side. Head towards the prominent white house on Pan Point. (This was built by the port contractor so that he could survey all his works, then became the coastguard station for many years. Now it is a private residence.)

If the weather is kind, turn out along the South Pier to the beacon that marks the mouth of the River Coquet

# Warkworth 28

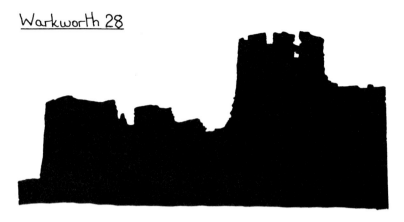

Other walks based on Warkworth include:

- <u>Warkworth Beach and the Mouth of Aln</u>. (details can be found in "Northumbrian Coastline"). Walk out to the beach and turn north along the beautiful sands, past Birling Carrs to the river, opposite Alnmouth.
Note that the Aln, in normal conditions, is only fordable here for about 1½ hours at low tide. If in doubt, don't!
To reach Alnmouth from there means a long diversion inland, including a stretch of the twisting, narrow and very busy A1068 road — not a place for walkers. Catch a bus back to Warkworth, or pleasurably retrace your steps.

- <u>Morwick</u>. To gain an impression of the beautiful and twisting Coquet Valley is not easy. No continuous riverside path exists between the Hermitage Ferry and Guyzance. But from the Ferry Landing you can go up over the hill, past Howlet Hall and the suburbia of Heather Leazes. A lane leads down to a ford and long footbridge, that lead across onto a peninsula almost cut off by a loop of the Coquet. On the far side of the loop (which suffers a prominent caravan site) is Morwick Crag, a cliff beside the river sporting ancient cup and ring markings. Further upstream, beyond the ford (no bridge, no stones - not for the timid), is picturesque Morwick Mill.

# Warkworth 29

Carrickfergus Tower

Come back again to Warkworth!

## Warkworth Index

| | | | |
|---|---|---|---|
| Amble | 24, 27 | Marina | 27 |
| ......... Braid | 26, 27 | Market Place | 9 |
| Beacon Hill | 24 | Morwick | 21, 23 |
| Book House | 11 | National School | 17 |
| Borough School | 17 | North Pier, Amble | 25 |
| Bridge | 6 | Pan Point | 27 |
| Bridge End House | 18 | Percys, Dukes of N'land | 4, 13, 23 |
| Bridge gatehouse | 7 | | |
| Bridge Street | 8 | Percy the Pelican | 17 |
| Burgages | 18 | Presbyterian Church | 17 |
| Butts | 16 | Queen Alexandra's Landing | 20 |
| Castle | 12-15, 21, 26 | St. Lawrence | 4 |
| Castle's Dike | 24 | South Pier, Amble | 27 |
| Castle Street | 10 | United Reformed Church. | 17 |
| Coquet Island | 15, 25, 26 | Warkworth Beach | 24 |
| Coquet Lodge | 21 | Bridge | 6 |
| Coquet Yacht Club | 27 | Castle | 12-15, 21, 26 |
| English Heritage | 12, 22 | Harbour | 24 |
| Hermitage | 20, 22-23 | Weir. | 26 |

The following books have been informative about Warkworth;

| | | | |
|---|---|---|---|
| County History of Northumberland, Vol 5. | | 1899, | (N.C.C.) |
| Northumberland, | N. Pevsner | 1957 | (Penguin) |
| Northumbria | E. Grierson | 1976 | (Collins) |
| Northumbrian Heritage, | N. Ridley | 1968 | (Robt Hale) |
| Portrait of Northumberland, N. Ridley | | 1965 | (Robt. Hale) |
| Highways and Byways in N'land, P. Anderson Graham | | 1920 | (Macmillan) |
| The Queen's England, N'land, A. Mee et al | | 1952 | (N'ld Ed.Cttee) |
| Companions into Northumberland, S. Moorhouse, | | 1953 | (Methuen) |
| Discovering Northumberland, T. H. Rowland, | | 1973 | (Frank Graham) |
| Mediaeval Castles, Towers, etc  T. H. Rowland | | 1987 | (T.H. Rowland). |
| Parish Church of St. Lawrence, Warkworth | | | |
| Warkworth Castle | | 1988 | (Eng. Heritage). |
| Warkworth Hermitage | | 1985 | (H.B.M.C.E.) |
| and | | | |
| Northumbrian Coastline, | I. Smith | 1988 | (Sandhill). |